READER'S DELIGHT

Biography of
Dr. C.V. Raman

READER'S DELIGHT

An Imprint of Ramesh Publishing House

NEW DELHI

ISBN 978-93-5012-260-0

Published by: Alok Kumar Gupta *for* Reader's Delight
(An Imprint of Ramesh Publishing House)

Admin. Office: 12-H, New Daryaganj Road, Opp. Traffic Kotwali,
New Delhi-110002 ☎ 23261567, 23275224 Telefax: 011-23275124

Showroom: ● 4457, Nai Sarak, Delhi-6 ☎ 23918938
● 2604, Balaji Market, Nai Sarak, Delhi-6 ☎ 23253720, 23282525

E-Mail: info@rameshpublishinghouse.com
Website: www.rameshpublishinghouse.com

PREFACE

The Biography of Dr. C.V. Raman is the life sketch of the most illustrious son of India who contributed immensely for the advancement of science in our country and the world. He discovered the 'Raman Effect' phenomenon which is named after him. He won the Nobel Prize in those days when India was not independent and the facilities for education, experiments and research were quite scarce. It was again a unique phenomenon of him that while doing his government job as an Assistant Accountant General, who had nothing to do with science in particular, he kept alive his love for science by burning midnight oil doing study, experiments and intensive research on his own initiative.

The inside pages consist of an exploring account of the life of a village boy who through his self-determination and burning desire to discover his passion went on studying and experimenting on his own and rose to become the first Indian and even the first Asian Scientist to win a Nobel Prize and secured his place among the legendary scientists of the world who founded the very basics of modern science.

—Publisher

CONTENTS

INTRODUCTION

"I am a man of Science."

—Dr. C.V. Raman

C.V. Raman is one of the most renowned scientists produced by India. His full name was Chandrasekhara Venkata Raman. For his pioneering work on scattering of light, C.V. Raman won the Nobel Prize for Physics in 1930.

Chandrasekhara Venkata Raman was born at Tiruchirapalli in Southern India on November 7, 1888. His father was a lecturer in mathematics and physics so from the very beginning, he was immersed in an academic atmosphere. C.V. Raman entered the Presidency College, Madras, in 1902, and in 1904 passed his Bachelors examination, winning the first place and the gold medal in Physics. In 1907, he gained his Masters degree, obtaining the highest distinctions.

His earliest researches in optics and acoustics, the two fields of investigation to which he has dedicated his entire career, were carried out while he was a student.

Raman wanted to go to England for further studies but he was declared physically unfit to go to England by the Civil Surgeon of Madras. Raman then joined the Indian Finance Department in 1907 after topping the Financial Civil Services (FCS) examination. Though the duties of his office took most of his time, Raman found opportunities for carrying on experimental research in the laboratory of the Indian Association for the Cultivation of Science at Calcutta (Kolkata) of which he became the Honorary Secretary in 1919.

In 1917, he was offered the newly endowed Palit Chair of Physics at Kolkata University, and decided to accept it. After 15 years at Calcutta, he became Professor at the Indian Institute of Science at Bangalore (1933–1948). Raman also founded the Indian Journal of Physics in 1926, of which he was the Editor. He sponsored the establishment of the Indian Academy of Sciences and served as president since its inception. He also initiated the proceedings of that academy, in which much of his work has been published.

In 1922, Raman published his work on the "Molecular Diffraction of Light", the first of a series of investigations with his collaborators which ultimately led to his discovery of the radiation effect on February 28, 1928 and gained him the 1930 Nobel Prize in Physics.

Other investigations carried out by Raman were his experimental and theoretical studies on the diffraction of light by acoustic waves of ultrasonic and hypersonic frequencies (published in 1934-1942), and those on the effects produced by X-rays on infrared vibrations in crystals exposed to ordinary light.

In 1948, Raman, through studying the spectroscopic behaviour of crystals, approached in a new manner the fundamental problems of crystal dynamics. His laboratory had been dealing with the structure and properties of diamond, the structure and optical behaviour of numerous iridescent substances. Among his other interests had been the optics of colloids, electrical and magnetic anisotropy, and the physiology of human vision.

Raman has been honoured with a large number of honorary doctorates and memberships of scientific societies. He was elected a Fellow of the Royal Society early in his career (1924), and was knighted in 1929. Dr. C.V. Raman died on November 21, 1970, at the age of eighty two.

— *** —

FAMILY HISTORY

Tiruchirapalli is a town on the banks of the river Cauvery. R. Chandrasekhara Iyer was a teacher in a school there. He was a scholar in Physics and Mathematics. He loved music. His wife was Parvathi Ammal. Their second son was

R. Chandrashekhar Iyer & Parvathi Ammal (Raman's parents)

born on 7th November 1888. They named the boy Venkata Raman. He was also called Chandrasekhara Venkata Raman or C.V. Raman.

Raman was three years old when his father joined the A.V.N. College at Vishakhapatnam, Andhra Pradesh, as lecturer in Mathematics and Physics. He had procured an excellent collection of books on Physics, Mathematics and Philosophy. Chandrasekhara Iyer was a great lover of music and played violin extremely well.

Raman looked very ordinary and quite unimpressive in his childhood but he had the brain of a genius.

— *** —

EDUCATION

Raman finished his schooling at a very young age of 11. He spent the next two years studying in his father's college. When he was barely 13, he went to Madras to join the B.A. course in Presidency college. Raman was failed to win a word of praise initially from his teachers. Besides being young in his class, Raman was also quite unimpressive in his appearance. He could recall the incident occurred during his first English class that he attended. Observing Raman, his English Professor E.H.Elliot asked him whether he really belonged to the junior B.A. class. Raman immediately answered him 'yes' in affirmative tone. By the end of the course, he stunned all the skeptics and stood first in the B.A. Examinations.

At 15, Raman passed his B.A. exam and got gold medals for Physics and for English. He passed his M.A. examination in 1907, at his age of 19. Being so young, it would surprise even his teachers to believe that this inconspicuous child could be a college student at all. His Professors in the Presidency College found him to be so knowledgeable, that they recognized that Raman did not need class-room instructions, and they exempted him from attending all science classes.

Raman was an extra-ordinary observer. At 16, while doing a routine experiment on his college spectrometer, he observed some diffraction bands. We all do these experiments, but rarely does anybody observes the findings critically, investigate the data, and analyze the same thoroughly. Raman's observations in that routine experiment constituted the subject of his first research paper, which was published by one of the most prestigious scientific journals of that time, namely, the Philosophical Magazine. In the very same issue, he published yet another article on a totally different topic: a short note on a new method he devised to measure a liquid's surface tension.

When Raman completed his B.A. education, it was suggested that he go to England for further studies and take up Indian Civil Services (ICS) examination. It was a very prestigious exam in those days and very rarely did non-Britishers get through it. Yet, Raman impressed his teachers so much that they urged him to take it up at a very early age. Despite of Raman's brilliance, the plan was not to work. Raman had to undergo a medical examination before he could qualify to take the ICS test, and the civil surgeon of Madras declared him medically unfit to travel to England. This was the only exam that Raman failed in his life. Later in his life, he remarked in his characteristic style about the man who disqualified him, "I shall ever be grateful to this man", but at that time, he simply put the attempt behind him and went on to study Physics. Subsequently, after he completed his M.A., he took the Civil Services competitive exam for the Finance Department (FCS). Sure enough, he topped the score in that exam.

— *** —

MARRIAGE

Raman had cleared his FCS examination at the age of 18 in 1907. Once, he saw a 13 years old girl playing a *Thyagaraja Keerthana* on the *Veena*. He was a great lover of music and was deeply impressed by her performance. Against all conventions of that time, he arranged his marriage with her. Her name was Lokasundari.

Loksundari (Raman's wife) with Kasturba Gandhi

The saying "there is always a woman behind every great man" is very true in Raman's life. Lady Lokasundari Raman was a wonderful wife and happily interested in mothering all her husband's students. But for her ever loving care and shouldering the unavoidable worries of the day to day existence, Professor Raman would hardly have been able to devote himself so wholeheartedly to scientific research.

In 1907, when Raman was just over 18 years old, he along with his wife went to Calcutta to join the Finance Department there as Assistant Accountant General. Within a week of his reaching Calcutta, he noticed, while he was on his way to work, a sign board which read "The Indian Association for Cultivation of Sciences", and this was to play a major role in his life, and in the very history of scientific culture in our country.

— *** —

LIVING ACCOUNTANT BREATHING SCIENCE

One evening Raman was returning from his office in a tramcar. He saw the name plate of the 'Indian Association for the Cultivation of Science' at 210, Bow Bazaar Street. Immediately he got off the tram and went in. Dr. Amritlal Sircar was the Honarary Secretary of the Association. There were spacious rooms and old scientific instruments, which could be used for demonstration of experiments.

Raman asked whether he could conduct research there in his spare time. Dr. Sircar gladly agreed. Raman took up a house adjoining the Association. A door was provided between his house and the laboratory. During the daytime he would attend his office and carry out his duties. His mornings and nights were devoted to research. This gave him full satisfaction. So he continued his ceaseless activities in Calcutta.

His work was interrupted by a transfer to Rangoon for about a year in 1909, and also to Nagpur, in 1910. At both these places, he continued his experiments at his residence, with limited, insignificant facilities. Fortunately, in 1911, he was transferred back to Calcutta and could continue his work at the Indian Association for Cultivation of Science.

Ever since Raman was part of the IACS, he played a dual role. He would work efficiently as a finance officer all the day, and after office hours, move to the IACS, where he would immerse himself in research until late night. During these years, his papers appeared in International journals such as Nature and Philosophical Magazine, published in England, and the Physical Review, published in the USA. He started communicating with the physicists round the world at this time. He also liked to teach and would give popular lectures in Calcutta. People loved his lectures as they would include live demonstrations that made even non-specialists understand his work.

— *** —

LOVE FOR WAVES & SOUNDS

At the Association, Raman worked on a large number of problems. He would get interested in everything he observed, and indeed, a very keen observer he was. He would then go into the roots and attempt to understand the mechanism which governed the observed phenomena. This is the very method of science, and it is extra-ordinary, even in the context of several giants of science this century has seen, that there would be very few scientists who have indulged in such a variety of research problems. Thus, Raman followed up the recitations he heard his father play on the violin by his papers on the bowed string, the struck string, the maintenance of vibrations, on resonance, the sounds of splashes, and on music from heated metals! This, by no means, is a complete list of his research interests even in the field of sound and music alone! He discovered the overtones in the sounds of the mridangam and the tabla, thoroughly analysed them, and showed how the richness of these percussion instruments is so much superior to the normal stretched membrane of the western drums. Raman, during that period, published a beautiful paper on the acoustical knowledge of the ancient Hindus, and had already become an international expert on sound and musical instruments.

Raman was fascinated by waves and sounds and always carried in his mind the memory of reading Helmholtz's book on 'The Sensations of Tone' in his school days. He got a chance to study and experiment in the IACS, he chose to study musical instruments first. He used an idea found in Helmholtz's book, he explained the working of the Ektara, which is a simple instrument made of a resonant box and a string stretched to lie across the cavity. Starting from his understanding of this simple object, he developed many ideas that he called 'remarkable resonances'. During this time, he took up the violin for study and developed a way of characterizing the quality the instrument. It was the first time a scientific understanding was established, and it is employed even today. Raman's studies on the violin were extensive and published as a book entitled 'On the Mechanical Theory of Musical Instruments of the Violin Family with Experimental Results: Part I".

Raman had excellent organizational capacity, and had a great vision for the future of science in India. He started a Bulletin of the Indian Association in which original results of the research done would be published. This Bulletin grew, in 1917, into a full science journal, known as the Indian Journal of Physics.

— *** —

BECOMING PALIT PROFESSOR

In 1917, Professor Ashutosh Mukherjee, who was the Vice Chancellor of the Calcutta University at that time, requested C.V. Raman to come out of his job at the Accounts Department and accept the prestigious Tarakanath Palit Professorship of Physics at the University of Calcutta. There was a hitch in Raman's appointment, however, since there was a regulation which required that a candidate for the Palit professorship must be trained in a foreign country. The self-respecting Raman refused to comply, and the distinguished Vice Chancellor happily changed the rules to appoint Raman.

While he was Palit Professor at the Calcutta University, in 1919, Professor Raman became the Honorary Secretary of the Indian Association for Cultivation of Sciences and thus had two laboratories to work with. In 1921, Raman went to Oxford as a delegate at the Universities' Congress. One nagging phenomenon keeps surfacing as we reflect on virtually any aspect of Raman's life. This is his extra-ordinary observational capacity, and his keenness, enthusiasm, and total competence to understand his observations. During this visit to Europe, he visited the Saint Paul's Cathedral whose whispering gallery is famous the world over. Raman's excitement at the whispering gallery went well beyond that of anybody who ever visited that Cathedral, for Raman did a few small experiments and analyzed the results. His findings were far from trivial, and were published in two research articles in two of the foremost science journals, one in 'Nature' and the other in the 'Proceedings of the Royal Society'.

— *** —

RAMAN AS PROFESSOR & TEACHER

In 1917, at the age of 29, Raman became the Palit Professor. He continued research along with the new assignment.

Raman was very deeply interested in musical instruments such as the Veena, the Violin, the Mridangam and the Tabala. He began to work on them. Around 1918, he explained the complex vibrations of the strings of musical instruments. He later found out the characteristic tones emitted by the Mridangam, the Tabla etc.

Amritlal Sircar, who was devoting all his time to the welfare of the Indian Association for the Cultivation of Science, passed away in 1919. Professor Raman then became its Honarary Secretary. Two laboratories - those of the College and of the Association - were under him; and this gave a new stimulus to his researches. Both his body and his mind could do all the work that had to be done. Many students came to him from different parts of the country for post-graduate studies and research. IACS and the University Science College Laboratory - these became the active research centers of India. Research workers like Meghnad Saha and S.K. Mitra, who became famous later, worked at these centres.

That was a time when Raman was completely immersed in experiments and research. According to the terms of the

Palit Chair, he could have remained free from teaching work, doing research only. But Raman had great pleasure in teaching. Students were inspired by his lectures. They were eager to listen to him. He would not stick to one particular textbook. His lectures brought the fragrance of fresh research. They reflected Raman's great curiosity about the secrets of nature. Usually the lecture was of an hour's duration. Forgetting the time in the discussion of the subject, Professor Raman would sometimes lecture for two or three hours. Any doubt or question from a student would stimulate new scientific ideas.

Professor Raman was not only a great investigator but also a great teacher in the true sense of the word. His ideas and personality attracted many young research students and he held their loyalty and affection by extending a never-failing friendship to them. He not only taught methods of scientific research to his students, but by his own example made them realize the necessity of endurance, steadiness and hard work in the pursuit of knowledge.

Absorbed in experiments, it was not unusual for him to forget food and sleep. Sometimes working late at night, he would sleep in the laboratory on one of the tables.

In the mornings too, most of his time was spent in the laboratory. He worked in informal clothes. At 9.30 a.m. he would rush home. After a shave and a bath he would dress up and send for a taxi.

He would finish his breakfast in two or three minutes and get into the taxi. Racing over a distance of four miles, he would reach the class on time. He never wasted time.

— *** —

THE SEA IS BLUE
THE RAMAN WAY

The University of Calcutta conferred on Raman an honorary doctorate in 1921. Soon after, he made his first visit to overseas. It was a formal visit to attend the University Congress at Oxford, where he represented Calcutta University. During his return journey to India, Raman spent hours watching the sea from the deck of his ship and was awe-struck by its colour. According to Lord Rayleigh, who had explained the blue colour of the sea, 'The dark blue of the deep sea has nothing to do with the colour of water but is simply the blue of the sky seen in reflection'. Fascinated by it, Raman watched the sea intently and using the simple optical tools he usually carries. He did experiments to capture the colour of the sea. When ship finally docked at Bombay, Raman's paper explaining his observations on the Mediterranean Sea was on its way to the journal Nature.

During his return journey, Raman discovered that water molecules could scatter light just like air molecules. It was very important and radical in those days. It paves way for Raman to discovering the famous Raman Effect. He wrote a brilliant essay in 1922, titled, "The Molecular Diffraction of Light", in which he speculated that light may exist in quanta, that is, massless particles of energy. This is an accepted theory till today but considered as the most radical in those days. This research further proved to be important in his later life and it brought laurels to his country. Raman had a hunch that if the light did not exist as particles, or quanta, then scattering experiments would show only a change in the light intensity and not in its frequency, or colour. On the other hand, if light did exist in particles, or quanta, then a scattering of the light could change its frequency as well as intensity. He moved forward, giving a deaf ear to what others say, directed all research at the institute towards finding evidence for the corpuscular theory of light through scattering experiments. However, in 1923, with the discovery of the Compton effect, the existence of light quanta was established beyond doubt. With this success, Raman directed his team to work on light scattering. Initially their research findings were weak, some of his students named their initial finding as 'feeble fluorescence'.

Raman's team had to work rigorously four more years to be sure of what experiment they were doing. It was in 1927, they were able to say confidently that the new effect was not 'a type of fluorescence' but a modified scattering. This led to the discovery made on 28 February of the fact that light can undergo a scattering through a liquid resulting in a change in its frequency – the famous Raman Effect. To commemorate this historic event, this date is celebrated today as National Science Day.

— *** —

THE RESEARCH CONTINUED

Professor Raman's work on the scattering of x-rays by liquids was also a pioneering one, and formed the basis of molecular structure studies in liquids. His paper along with collaborator Ramanathan has become extremely famous, and was a pioneering contribution made as early as in 1923. In the same year, Professor Raman advanced a theory of viscosity which has been used to explain the viscosity of polymers.

Raman demonstrating his work

In 1924, Professor Raman was elected as a Fellow of the Royal Society. At the meeting that was held to felicitate him, he expressed his appreciation for the honour he received. However, he went on to say that he did not consider this honour to be the ultimate and that he would, within 5 years, get the Nobel Prize for India. This confidence, determination, working toward specific goals, was characteristic of Raman's personality. It can certainly be argued that after all it could have been a matter of chance that he would not get the Nobel Prize, it may also be said that Raman had a fair idea of his research caliber.

In 1922, Professor Raman published a monograph entitled "The Molecular Diffraction of Light". The seeds of his subsequent work can be found in this work. In this monograph, for example, he has considered in details how energy could be transferred between a quantum of light and a molecule of liquid. He had expressed his conviction in this celebrated monograph, that the quantum nature of light must manifest itself in molecular scattering.

—— *** ——

RAMAN DISCOVERS RAMAN EFFECT

In the month of April 1923, Professor Raman's distinguished student, K.R.Ramanathan, initiated some experiments on the scattering of light by water. The experiment was done using sunlight, and the scattered light was seen as a track in the transverse direction, and using a system of filters, the scattered light was examined. The filters were arranged in such a way that when the incident light was passed through one of the two complementary filters and the scattered light was viewed through the other filter, no track should have been

Raman with his spectrometer

visible at all. Some track however could be observed, and was attributed to a weak fluorescence of the impurity molecules. Ramanathan himself wrote later that it was Professor Raman himself, and none other, who was not satisfied by the explanation based on the fluorescence model and that he (Raman) wondered if the track observed was due to some characteristic molecular scattering. The same effect was observed later in many organic liquids by K.S.Krishnan, another of Raman's distinguished students.

There was a certain similarity in the explanation Raman had in mind with that of what is known as the Compton Effect. In the winter of 1927, Professor Raman went to Waltair for a short visit; he derived a formula for molecular scattering now known as the Compton-Raman formula.

In January 1928, another associate of Professor Raman, Venkateswaran, observed that in pure glycerin, the scattered light was greenish in color, instead of the usual blue. Moreover, the radiation was strongly polarized. In the last week of January, Professor Raman asked K.S. Krishnan to repeat these experiments under more carefully controlled conditions.

K.S. Krishnan was at that time doing completely theoretical work and Professor Raman advised him that it was not healthy for a man of science to stay out of touch with actual experiments for any significant length of time. Krishnan also reported the same type of findings as Ramanathan did, and Professor Raman personally verified all the observations.

Professor Raman was extremely excited about the findings, since he understood exactly what this just discovered phenomenon was. On 16th February, Raman sent a note to *Nature*, suggesting that the modified radiation observed in these scattering experiments could be due to certain molecular fluctuations. Yet, however, the phenomenon was not fully understood. On the 27th February,

Raman set up an experiment in which he decided to view the track earlier thought to be due to fluorescence using a direct vision spectroscope. The experiment could not be completed that evening, as by the time the experiment was set up, the sun had set. Next morning, February 28th, 1928, when the experiment was done personally by Professor Raman, he found that the track contained not only the incident color but also another one separated by a dark region. This was the very first observation of what is known as the Raman Effect.

An announcement was made to the Associated Press on 29th February (in the leap year) and Professor Raman sent a note to Nature on March 8th announcing his discovery along with a complete explanation.

The Raman Effect, first announced in the Indian Journal of Physics in 1928, was named by the Royal Society of London as "among the best three or four discoveries in experimental physics of the decade." The discovery not only opened up a new branch of spectroscopy, it has contributed enormously to our knowledge of the structure and dynamics of molecules and crystals. Recently, the Raman Effect has been exploited in the design of masers and lasers, to make available more frequencies than would otherwise be possible. The fact that nearly 10,000 papers have been published so far on Raman Effect and allied phenomena from all over the world speaks for itself of the importance of the discovery.

— ∗∗∗ —

THE RAMAN EFFECT ON THE WORLD

Several laboratories in the world, on coming to know of this experiment, repeated such measurements and confirmed the findings. The recognition that followed in terms of the Nobel prize was almost inevitable, despite the fact that Raman was an Indian. The Nobel prize for Physics is given each year at Stockholm, Sweden, on the 10th of December, and the award is announced for that year about a month in advance. The Nobel committee meetings are held in great secrecy and between the time of announcement and the award ceremony, it would be very difficult to manage a journey to Sweden at such a short notice. Raman, however, made the trip, as even before the award was announced, he had already booked 2 tickets on a steamer, for himself and for his wife.

The Raman effect involves an exchange of a quantum of energy between a molecule and the electromagnetic radiation. Molecular energy levels are quantized, and this means that a molecule cannot possess an arbitrary amount of energy. The energy may be due to various reasons, and one may thus speak of the electronic energy, rotational energy or the vibrational energy of the molecule. A molecule may undergo transition from one energy state to another only by absorbing or emitting a discrete amount of energy. Raman Spectroscopy involves the study of such transitions. This is now an extremely specialized branch of spectroscopy and has undergone enormous developments. Raman spectroscopy is rarely done using sunlight as a source.

Now, Laser radiation is employed and it has very many fascinating applications, and the technique is known as the Laser-Raman Spectroscopy.

— *** —

RAMAN : A WORLD CLASS SCIENTIST

Scientists of many countries appreciated the research papers of Raman and his colleagues. The Royal Society, the oldest and the most important science society of England, honoured Raman in 1924 by electing him as its 'Fellow' (that is, a member).

The annual session of 'The British Association for the Cultivation of Science' was held in the same year in Toronto (Canada). Raman inaugurated the seminar on the scattering of light. R.A. Millikan, the famous American Physicist, who also attended, was full of admiration for Raman. They became fast friends too.

At the Mount Wilson Observatory in California (U.S.A), a telescope of 100-inch width was in use. Those were the times when discoveries in the field of astronomy (study of stars and planets and their movements) filled people with wonder. Raman was always eager to learn new things. He spent a couple of days on Mount Wilson. During the nights he viewed the Nebula (bright or dark patch in the sky caused by distant stars or a cloud of gas or dust) through the telescope and was thrilled.

He went to Russia in 1925 to participate in the two hundredth anniversary of the 'Russian Academy of Sciences'.

— *** —

THE RAMAN EFFECT

Sometimes a rainbow appears and delights our eyes. We see in it shades of red, orange, yellow, green, blue, indigo and violet. The white ray of the sun includes all these colors. When a beam of sunlight is passed through a glass prism a patch of these color-bands are seen. This is called the spectrum. The Spectrometer is an apparatus used to study the spectrum. Spectral lines in it are characteristic of the light passing through the prism. A beam of light that causes a single spectral line is said to be monochromatic.

When a beam of monochromatic light passes through a transparent substance (a substance which allows light to pass through it), the beam is scattered. Raman spent a long time in the study of the scattered light. On February 28, 1928, he observed two low intensity spectral line corresponding to the incident mono-chromatic light. Years of his labour had borne fruit. It was clear that though the incident light was monochromatic, the scattered light due to it, was not monochromatic.Thus Raman's experiments discovered a phenomenon which was lying hidden in nature.

The 16th of March 1928 is a memorable day in the history of science. On that day a meeting was held under the joint auspices of the South Indian Science Association and the Science Club of Central College, Bangalore; Raman was the Chief Guest. He announced the new phenomenon discovered by him to the world. He also acknowledged with affection the assistance given by K.S. Krishnan and Venkateshwaran, who were his students.

The phenomenon attracted the attention of research workers all over the world. It became famous as the 'Raman Effect'. The spectral lines in the scattered light were known as 'Raman Lines'.

Is light wave-like or particle-like? This question has been discussed from time to time by scientists. The Raman Effect confirmed that light was made up of particles known as 'photons'. It helped in the study of the molecular and crystal structures of different substances.

Investigations making use of the Raman Effect began in many countries. During the first twelve years after its discovery, about 1800 research papers were published on various aspects of it and about 2500 chemical compounds were studied. Raman Effect was highly praised as one of the greatest discoveries of the third decade of this century.

After the 'lasers' (devices that produce intense beams of light, their name coming from the initial letters of Light Amplification by Stimulated Emission of Radiation) came into use in the 1960s, it became easier to get monochromatic light of very high intensity for experiments. This brought back scientific interest in Raman Effect, and the interest remains alive to this day.

— *** —

HONOURS & NOBEL PRIZE

Raman received many honours from all over the world for his achievement. In 1928 the Science Society of Rome awarded the Matteucci Medal. In 1929 the British Government knighted him; thereafter Professor Raman came to be known as Professor Sir C.V. Raman. The Royal Society of London awarded the Hughes Medal in 1930. Honorary doctorate degrees were awarded by the Universities of Freiburg (Germany), Glasgow (England), Paris (France), Bombay, Benaras, Dacca, Patna, Mysore and several others.

The highest award a scientist or a writer can get is the Nobel Prize. In 1930, the Swedish Academy of Sciences chose Raman to receive the Nobel Prize for Physics. No Indian and no Asian

Dr. C.V. Raman with other Nobel Laureates of 1930, after the presentation of the prizes in Stockholm.

had received the Nobel Prize for Physics up to that time. At the ceremony for the award, Raman used alcohol to demonstrate the Raman Effect. Later in the evening alcoholic drinks were served at the dinner. But Raman did not touch them. He remained loyal to the Indian traditions.

Raman used to announce his new scientific discoveries at the annual sessions of the Academy. At the Madras session (1967) he discussed the influence of the earth's rotation on its gaseous envelope. Next year he put forward his theory of the physiology of vision. Many countries and institutions continued to honour him. The membership of the American Optical Society (1941), the National Professorship of India (1948), the Franklin Medal of the Franklin Institute (1951), the International Lenin Prize (1957), the Membership of the Pontifical Academy of Science (1961)—these were some of the honours conferred on him.

The greatest honour the Government of India confers on an Indian is the award of 'Bharat Ratna'. Raman became a 'Bharat Ratna' in 1954.

— ✳✳✳ —

THE STORY OF THE NOBEL PRIZE

The Nobel prize is one of the prizes known to a great part of the non-scientific public and is considered as the highest honour to be awarded to scientists.

Raman received the Nobel prize in a record time of two years after his prize-winning discovery.

In 1929, C. Fabry from Paris recommended J. Cabannes (Montpellier) and C. V. Raman (Calcutta), whereas N. Bohr proposed that either R. W. Wood or R. W. Wood and Raman should be considered for receiving the Nobel prize for physics. In that year 48 nominators sent 97 proposals and proposed in all 29 persons. Out of these 29 persons, L. de Broglie, Cabannes, Raman and Wood were declared by the Committee as the persons who fundamentally deserved the prize; but it was L. de Broglie who finally received the Prize for that year.

For the year 1930, 39 competent persons were asked to submit proposals. Out of them, 37 persons sent proposals. There were 21 valid recommendations for a full or shared Prize. Most of the recommendations were concerned with atomic theory and atomic physics. The atomic theory proposals had been worked out by Oseen.

Out of the 21 nominations, Raman was the most suitable person; he was proposed 10 times, either as a single candidate for the Prize, or to share it with other physicists.

In that year some of the other scientists proposed included, M. Born, A. Sommerfeld, E. Schrödinger, W. Heisenberg, H. F. Osborn, and M. N. Saha (an Indian astrophysicist).

Dr. C.V. Raman received the Nobel prize for his work on diffusion of light and for the effect named after him. The objections raised by some historians that Raman did not share the Nobel prize with others or that the Committee ignored Raman's collaborators as well as Russian colleagues were baseless. As he was awarded the Prize not only for the Raman effect, but for other work in this field as well. The Nobel Committee had to take the decision according to certain rules and regulations imposed on it by the Nobel Foundation. Raman was nominated 10 times and the nominators wrote convincing recommendations in favour of him; thus the Committee decided for Raman. He received the Nobel prize in record time due the practical significance of the discovery, as well as the good opinion of the famous contemporary scientists about his work.

— ✳✳✳ —

NOBEL PRIZE PRESENTATION SPEECH

Presentation Speech by Professor H. Pleijel, Chairman of the Nobel Committee for Physics of the Royal Swedish Academy of Sciences, on December 10, 1930.
Your Majesty, Your Royal Highnesses, Ladies and Gentlemen.

The Academy of Sciences, has resolved to award the Nobel Prize in Physics for 1930 to Sir Venkata Raman for his work on the scattering of light and for the discovery of the effect named after him.

The diffusion of light is an optical phenomenon, which has been known for a long time. A ray of light is not perceptible unless it strikes the eye directly. If, however, a bundle of rays of light traverses a medium in which extremely fine dust is present, the ray of light will scatter to the sides and the path of the ray through the medium will be discernible from the side. We can represent the course of events in this way; the small particles of dust begin to oscillate owing to electric influence from the ray of light, and they form centres from which light is disseminated in all directions. The wavelength, or the number of oscillations per second, in the light thus diffused is here the same as in the original ray of light. But this effect has different degrees of strength for light with different wavelengths. It is stronger for the short wavelengths than for the long ones, and consequently it is stronger for the blue part of the spectrum than for the red part. Hence if a ray of light containing all the colours of the spectrum passes through a medium, the yellow and the red rays will pass through the medium without appreciable scattering, whereas the blue rays will be scattered to the sides. This effect has received the name of the "Tyndall effect".

Lord Rayleigh, who has made a study of this effect, has put forward the hypothesis that the blue colours of the sky and the reddish colouring that is observed at sunrise and sunset is caused by the diffusion of light owing to the fine dust or the particles of water in the atmosphere. The blue light from the sky would thus be light-scattered to the sides, while the reddish light would be light that passes through the lower layers of the atmosphere and which has become impoverished in blue rays owing to scattering. Later, in 1899, Rayleigh threw out the suggestion that the phenomenon in question might be due to the fact that the molecules of air themselves exercised a scattering effect on the rays of light.

In 1914, Cabannes succeeded in showing experimentally that pure and dustless gases also have the capacity of scattering rays of light.

But a closer examination of scattering in different substances in solid, liquid, or gaseous form showed that the scattered light did not in certain respects exactly follow the laws which, according to calculation, should hold good for the Tyndall effect. The hypothesis which formed the basis of this effect would seem to involve, amongst other things, that the rays scattered to the sides were polarized. This, however, did not prove to be exactly the case.

This divergence from what was to be expected was made the starting point of a searching study of the nature of scattered light, in which study Raman was one of those who took an active part. Raman sought to find the explanation of the anomalies in asymmetry observed in the molecules. During these studies of his in the phenomenon of scattering, Raman made, in 1928, the unexpected and highly surprising discovery that the scattered light showed not only the radiation that derived from the primary light but also a radiation that contained other wavelengths, which were foreign to the primary light.

In order to study more closely the properties of the new rays, the primary light that was emitted from a powerful mercury lamp was filtered in such a way as to yield a primary light of one single wavelength. The light scattered from that ray in a medium was watched in a spectrograph, in which every wavelength or frequency produces a line. Here he found that, in addition to the mercury line chosen, there was obtained a spectrum of new sharp lines, which appeared in the spectrograph on either side of the original line. When another mercury line was employed, the same extra spectrum showed itself round it. Thus, when the primary light was moved, the new spectrum followed, in such a way that the frequency distance between the primary line and the new lines always remained the same.

Raman investigated the universal character of the phenomenon by using a large number of substances as a scattering medium, and everywhere found the same effect.

The explanation of this phenomenon, which has received the name of the "Raman effect" after its discoverer, has been found by Raman himself, with the help of the modern conception of the nature of light. According to that conception, light cannot be emitted from or absorbed by material otherwise than in the form of definite amounts of energy or what are known as "light quanta". Thus the energy of light would possess a kind of atomic character. A quantum of light is proportionate to the frequency of rays of light, so that in the case of a frequency twice as great, the quanta of the rays of light will also be twice as great.

In order to illustrate the conditions when an atom emits or absorbs light energy, we can, according to Bohr, picture to ourselves the atom as consisting of a nucleus, charged with positive electricity round which negative electrons rotate in circular paths at various distances from the centre. The path of every such electron possesses a certain energy, which is different for different distances from the central body.

Only certain paths are stable. When the electron moves in such a path, no energy is emitted. When, on the other hand, an electron falls from a path with higher energy to one with lower energy–that is to say, from an outer path to an inner path–light is emitted with a frequency that is characteristic of these two paths, and the energy of radiation consists of a quantum of light. Thus the atom can give rise to as many frequencies as the number of different transitions between the stable paths. There is a line in the spectrum corresponding to each frequency.

An incoming radiation cannot be absorbed by the atom unless its light quantum is identical with one of the light quanta that the atom can emit.

Now the Raman effect seems to conflict with this law. The positions of the Raman-lines in the spectrum do not correspond, in point of fact, with the frequencies of the atom itself, and they move with the activating ray. Raman has explained this apparent contradiction and the coming into existence of the lines by the effect of combination between the quantum of light coming from without and the quanta of light that are released or bound in the atom. If the atom, at the same time as it receives from without a quantum of light, emits a quantum of light of a different magnitude, and if the difference between these two quanta is identical with the quantum of light which is bound or released when an electron passes from one path to another, the quantum of light coming from without is absorbed. In that case the atom will emit an extra frequency, which either will be the sum of or the difference between the activating ray and a frequency in the atom itself. In this case these new lines group themselves round the incoming primary frequency on either side of it, and the distance between the activating frequency and the nearest Raman-lines will be identical with the lowest oscillation frequencies of the atom or with its ultrared spectrum. What has been said as to the atom and its oscillations also holds good of the molecule.

In this way we get the ultrared spectrum moved up to the spectral line of the activating light. The discovery of the Raman-line has proved to be of extraordinarily great importance for our knowledge of the structure of molecules.

So far, indeed, there have been all but insuperable difficulties in the way of studying these ultrared oscillations, because that part of the spectrum lies so far away from the region where the photographic plate is sensitive. Raman's discovery has now overcome these difficulties, and the way has been opened for the investigation of the oscillations of the nucleus of the molecules. We choose the primary ray within that range of frequency where the photographic plate is sensitive. The ultrared spectrum, in the form of the Raman-lines, is moved up to that region and, in consequence of that, exact measurements of its lines can be effected.

In the same way the ultraviolet spectrum can be investigated with the help of the Raman effect. Thus we have obtained a simple and exact method for the investigation of the entire sphere of oscillation of the molecules.

Raman himself and his fellow-workers have, during the years that have elapsed since the discovery was made, investigated the frequencies in a large number of substances in a solid, liquid, and gaseous state. Investigations have been made as to whether different conditions of aggregation affect atoms and molecules, and the molecular conditions in electrolytic dissociation and the ultrared absorption spectrum of crystals have been studied.

Thus the Raman effect has already yielded important results concerning the chemical constitution of substances; and it is to foresee that the extremely valuable tool that the Raman effect has placed in our hands will in the immediate future bring with it a deepening of our knowledge of the structure of matter.

Sir Venkata Raman, the Royal Academy of Sciences has awarded you the Nobel Prize in Physics for your eminent researches on the diffusion of gases and for your discovery of the effect that bears your name. 'The Raman Effect' has opened new routes to our knowledge of the structure of matter and has already given most important results.

I now ask you to receive the prize from the hands of His Majesty.

— *** —

RAMAN AT TATA INSTITUTE

Dr. Raman came to Bangalore as the Director of the Tata Institute (the Indian Institute of Science) in 1933. The Tata Institute soon became famous for the study of crystals. The diffraction of light (the very slight bending of light around corners) by ultrasonic waves (high frequency sound waves which we cannot hear) in a liquid was elegantly explained by Raman and Nagendranath. This became known as the 'Raman-Nath Theory'.

Raman was an early riser and used to take morning walks regularly. The sight of tall trees against the sky at dawn delighted him. By six in the morning he would be in the chamber where he worked. Up to 9 a.m. he would devote his time to discussion with students who were experimenting and to the study of research papers. At 10 o'clock he would be in the Director's office. He would complete the office work and return to the laboratory. He would be immersed in research till 8.30 p.m. He used to arrange two or three seminars every week. At these seminars all the workers would come together to discuss various problems of their research.

— *** —

RAMAN EFFECT ON BRAIN DRAIN

One event shows the extra-ordinary pride Raman felt as an Indian. Very many years later, when Raman had received worldwide recognition, there was an event. This was around 1933, when Raman was in Bangalore as the Director of what is now the Indian Institute of Science, then known as the Tata Institute. At that time, several German Physicists were fleeing their country to escape the atrocities committed by Hitler. Raman, who was opposed to young Indians going abroad for education, rather believed in getting great international stalwarts here. So he approached several of the German Physicists who were fleeing Germany and tried to attract them to take up permanent jobs in India.

Amongst the persons he approached are distinguished Physicists like Erwin Schrödinger and Max Born, both Nobel laureates. Unfortunately, as Schrödinger himself wrote in a letter, he had already accepted a job at Dublin when Raman's invitation reached him. Schrodinger also wrote in that letter, that he regretted that he could not settle in India, the land of the *Upanishads*.

— *** —

ENCOURAGING SCIENCE & RESEARCH

After retirement from the Indian Institute of Science in 1948 he started an Institute of his own with the sponsorship of the Indian Academy of Sciences which he had founded in 1935, in the hope that it would "become an international cultural center that would shown India's greatness in the field of exact sciences." The Raman Institue, besides being well equipped for research in the fields of spectroscopy, optics, X-rays, crystal physics and mineralogy, houses an outstanding museum attached to the Institute containing a magnificent collection of rocks and minerals, and possibly the largest collection in the world today of diamonds for experimental investigations.

The Government of Mysore granted 24 acres of land to promote the activities of the Academy. It was his earnest desire 'to bring into existence a centre of scientific research worthy of our ancient country, where the keenest intellectuals of our land can probe into the mysteries of the Universe'. He fulfilled his wish by establishing a Research Institute at Hebbal, Bangalore. He did not seek help from the Government but gave away all his property to the Institute. The Executive Committee of the Academy named the centre 'Raman Research Institute'.

In 1948, this great scientist entered on one more active phase of life when he became the Director of the Raman

Research Institute. The Institute became the centre of all his activities. A garden and tall eucalyptus trees surrounded it. He used to say, "A Hindu is required to go to the forest in old age, but instead of going to the forest, I made the forest come to me." At the Institute he could concentrate on things that interested him. He was alone with his work and was happy.

He did research on sound, light, rocks, gems, birds, insects, butterflies, sea shells, trees, flowers, atmosphere, weather and physiology of vision and hearing. His study covered such different fields of science as Physics, Geology, Biology and Physiology. Among them sound and colours particularly attracted him. Once he even went round shops to select sarees of different colour designs.

His interests in later years were mainly focused on finding a satisfactory explanation of the floral colours and the physiology of human vision. For his continued and relentless pursuit of science, honours continued to pour in. In 1941 he was awarded the Franklin medal, the title 'Bharat Ratna', the highest honour by India is 1954, the Lenin Prize in 1957, elected as an honorary fellow of the Optical Society of America, foreign Associate of the French Academy, corresponding member of the Russian Academy of Sciences, member of the Pointificial Academy of Sciences by the Pope in 1961, fellow of the Mineralogical Society of America, and memberships in numerous other scientific societies throughout the world.

— *** —

RAMAN : ORIGINAL THINKER & READER

Dr. C.V. Raman was one of the world renowned scientists of India. He was a brilliant, industrious and disciplined student. He was also an original thinker. During his youth, India was not a free country, and there were hardly any institutions or libraries to encourage for higher education. Despite these hurdles, Raman was able to contribute so greatly to Indian science. It was possible only because of his deep and genuine passion for physics and his commitment to finding answers to questions that puzzled him.

Raman was an intelligent and voracious reader and pored eagerly over all the books in his father's collection. Some among those were the original writings of the outstanding scientists. He once said, "out of this welter of subjects and books, can I pick anything really mould my mental and spiritual outlook and determine my chosen path? Yes, I can and shall mention three books."

"They are Edwin Arnold's 'Light of Asia' which is the life story of Lord Gautama Buddha. Second is 'The Elements of Euclid', is a treatise on Classical Geometry. 'The Sensations of Tone' is the last one and is authored by German scientist Helmholtz, on the properties of sound waves."

— ✳✳✳ —

47

RAMAN — THE DOWN TO EARTH MAN

Dr. Raman was greatly studious. He kept in touch with the latest developments in science in the world around him. He had personal contact with many scientists. He used to read new books and research papers from different centres. On one occasion he was addressing the students of Presidency College, Madras. Like an elder brother he told them, "How much can you learn in an hour's lecture? Spend more time in the library." Studying and experimenting, he remained a student throughout his life.

"The equipment which brought me the Nobel Prize did not cost more than three hundred rupees. A table drawer can hold all my research equipments," he used to say with pride. It was his conviction that if the research worker is not inspired from within, any amount of money cannot bring success in research.

He hoped that scientists of free India would win worldwide fame by their discoveries. "If there are no facilities here, what is wrong with their going abroad and spreading the fame of India? Did not the workers of the East India Company come and rule India?" he used to say.

Raman was not conservative in his outlook. He used to spell out his opinions boldly. When he was called

'India's illustrious scientist',! he would correct the description with humility—"I am just a man of science." When scientists were criticized, he would retort with confidence that they were the salt of the earth.

His greatness lay not just in his specialized field of research but in his extent of knowledge, his eagerness to collect and read books on other subjects in literature, music, science, and technology. His lectures to a lay audience made him especially noteworthy. He could capture the attention of school children, college students, and town people equally well. Possessing in a rare measure the extraordinary gift of making the most difficult problems in physics appear simple and with a keen and irresistible sense of humor, he would have the audience roaring in laughter every few minutes.

RAMAN — A FRUITFUL LIFE

Raman possessed the curiosity of a little boy to know new things, and the intuition of a great genius in understanding the secrets of Nature. The life of this great scientist was truly the life of a great seer.

Without much encouragement, Raman had entered the field of science in his early years. Deeply attracted by the secrets of sound and light, he marched ahead in the world of science. By his achievements and self-respect he earned a honored place for India in the world of science. He laid the foundations of a scientific tradition in India by building up institutes for research, by publishing science journals and by encouraging young scientists.

Raman exhibited remarkable independence in choosing to work in areas that exited his curiosity. Further, when faced with lack of infrastructure, he always improvised and built up whatever he needed from scratch. C.V. Raman's determination, spirit, and contributions indeed remain special within the context of the practice of science in India.

Raman took over Indian Institute of Science, Bangalore as a Director and he stayed there until 1948. He spent equal amount of time on research and organizational work.

He not only conducted research but also mentored many students.

Raman dedicated his final years from 1948 to 1970, to set up of the Raman Research Institute in Bangalore and the running of the Indian Academy of Science. Despite his busy schedule, he edited journals 'Current Science' and the 'Proceedings of the Academy'.

A few days before his 83rd birthday, Raman suffered a mild heart attack. But there was quick recovery. He never dreamt of a life without work. When advised rest, he told his doctor, "I wish to live a hundred-per-cent active and fruitful life."

Dr. C.V. Raman died on 21 November, 1970. By a special arrangement, according to his wish, his mortal remains were consigned to flames in the institute campus itself, amidst the surroundings he loved, without any religious ceremonies. Today, a solitary tree is all that marks that spot in the grounds of the Raman Research Institute.

— *** —

DR. RAMAN IN DIFFERENT PERSPECTIVES

Raman's Delight in Colour and Light

Raman collected rocks and precious stones. His invaluable collection included hundreds of objects such as sand that melted due to lightning, rock indicating the lava flow during a volcano and diamonds, rubies and sapphires. Many fluorescent minerals were kept in a dark room. There he could create a small twinkling world by switching on the ultra-violet light. Thin layers of some crystals were prepared for study. No colour was seen when they were viewed perpendicularly. But the viewer had only to change the angle—and blue, green and yellow colours delighted the eye. After a deep study of diamonds Raman explained many of their characteristics.

Once in Paris, he went shopping for diamonds and crystals. There two beautiful butterflies with blue wings in a shop window attracted him. He bought them and later collected thousands of specimens.

Raman loved flowers for their colours. He grew many flower plants. He used to visit flower exhibitions to examine flowers.

Raman's Interest in Music

Raman was a great lover of music. He used to say, "I should live long, because I have not heard all the music

I want to hear." He was a frequent visitor to a shop selling musical instruments in Balepet, in Bangalore. He collected a variety of musical instruments like the Mridangam, the Tabla, the Veena, the Violin and the Nagaswaram.

'The Catgut Acoustical Society' of America is devoted exclusively to the study of violins. It elected Raman as its honorary member.

Raman — 'A General Practitioner in Science'

When Raman stepped into the field of research, Modern Physics was in its infancy. It developed numerous branches by the time he began working in his own Institute. Then research workers had access to modern equipment and methods, which were not available six decades earlier. They tended to study a small field and to specialize in it. But Raman never limited his activities and interests to a narrow field.

Raman once inaugurated the 'General Practitioners' Conference' in Bangalore. A general practitioner is a doctor who treats common illnesses. Raman humorously commented on that occasion that he was a general practitioner in science. He liked all scientific problems whether they were small or big. His interest and satisfaction lay in finding a solution to the problem.

In 1969, the daughter of Nagendranath (who had been a research student under him thirty years earlier) was married; Raman and his wife attended the reception. Raman drew Nagendranath aside and explained his new problem; he was trying to find a theory of earthquakes taking into account the actual shape of the earth and the wave-like nature of the quakes. Raman was not a person to be satisfied with his past achievements. He was always seeking new and vaster fields of study.

Raman was a delightful speaker. Sprinkled with good humor, his talk was usually focussed on realities. Raman used to say that the colour of the sea interested him more than the fish, which lived in it. He thought that we should have our own ships for oceanographic research. He often said that India lost her freedom because she took no interest in the seas.

Raman had A Lion's Heart

Friends and admirers organized a special function at the Annual Session of the Academy at Ahmedabad to honour him on his eightieth birthday. Many people expressed warm sentiments. Raman never took much interest in birthday celebrations. Still, at the end, He thanked the organizers; and with a twinkle in his eyes, he said, "I wish some one had said that I had a lion's heart!" All who had spoken forgot to make mention of his great asset, namely courage.

Raman's God and Religion

Raman would not speak much about God and religion. Science was his God and work his religion. He believed that new discoveries confirm the existence of God; if there is God we have to find Him in this universe.

A journalist once asked him, "What do you feel about the long and eventful period of your scientific work and achievements?" Raman replied promptly, "I have no time to think of the past and I am not inclined to do so. I spend my life as a scientist. My work gives me satisfaction."

— *** —

CHRONOLOGY OF EVENTS

- Birth of C.V. Raman : 7 November, 1888
- Done Matric : 1902
- Done B.A. : 1905
- Done M.A. : 1907
- Joined the FCS at Calcutta : 1907
- Marriage : 6 May, 1907
- Joined IACS at Calcutta : 1907
- Transferred to Rangoon : 1909
- Father Passed Away : 1910
- Became Palit Professor at Calcutta University : 1917
- Became Honorary Secretary of IACS : 1919
- Went to England to represent Calcutta University : 1921
- Honoured as fellow of the Royal Society : 1924
- Visited Canada & America : 1924
- Went to Russia : 1925
- Found Raman-Effect : 16th March, 1928
- Attained Knighthood : 1929
- Received Nobel Prize : 1930
- Joined Tata Institute, Bangalore : 1933
- Established the Indian Academy of Science : 1934
- Established The Raman Research Institute : 1948
- Conferred Bharat Ratna : 1954
- Passed Away : 21 Nov., 1970

— *** —

SOME RARE PHOTOGRAPHS

Dr. Raman with Dr. Zakir Hussain

Dr. C.V. Raman with his wife Loksundari

Dr. Raman and Dr. Rajendra Prasad

Dr. C.V. Raman with Soviet physicists

Dr. Raman with Jawaharlal Nehru

Dr. Raman with Mahatma Gandhi